Robyn O'Sullivan

Contents

What Is a Cave?

A cave is a hole or space underground that has an **entrance** on the surface. There are lots of amazing things to find out about caves. In this book you will explore different kinds of caves.

Some caves are in rocky cliffs or hillsides. Others are below the ground or in the sea. Let's find out how caves are formed and take a look at some different caves from around the world.

How Are Caves Formed?

It can take thousands of years for a cave to **form**. Sometimes it takes millions of years. Let's find out how it happens.

Some caves are formed by rainwater.

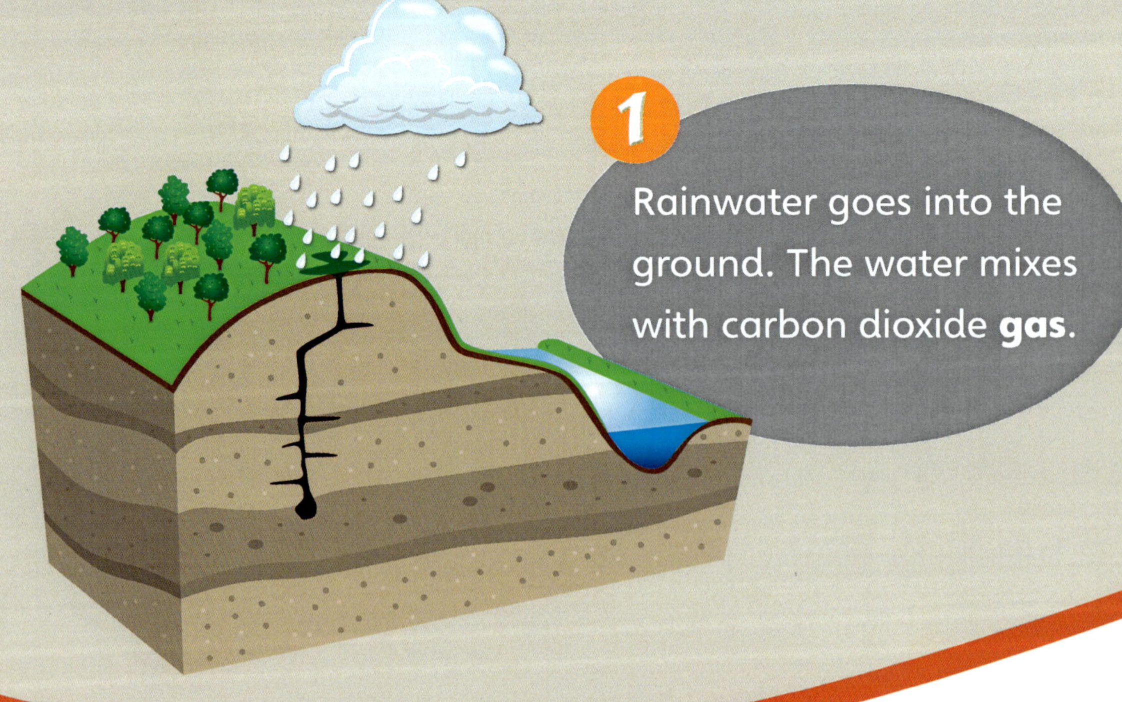

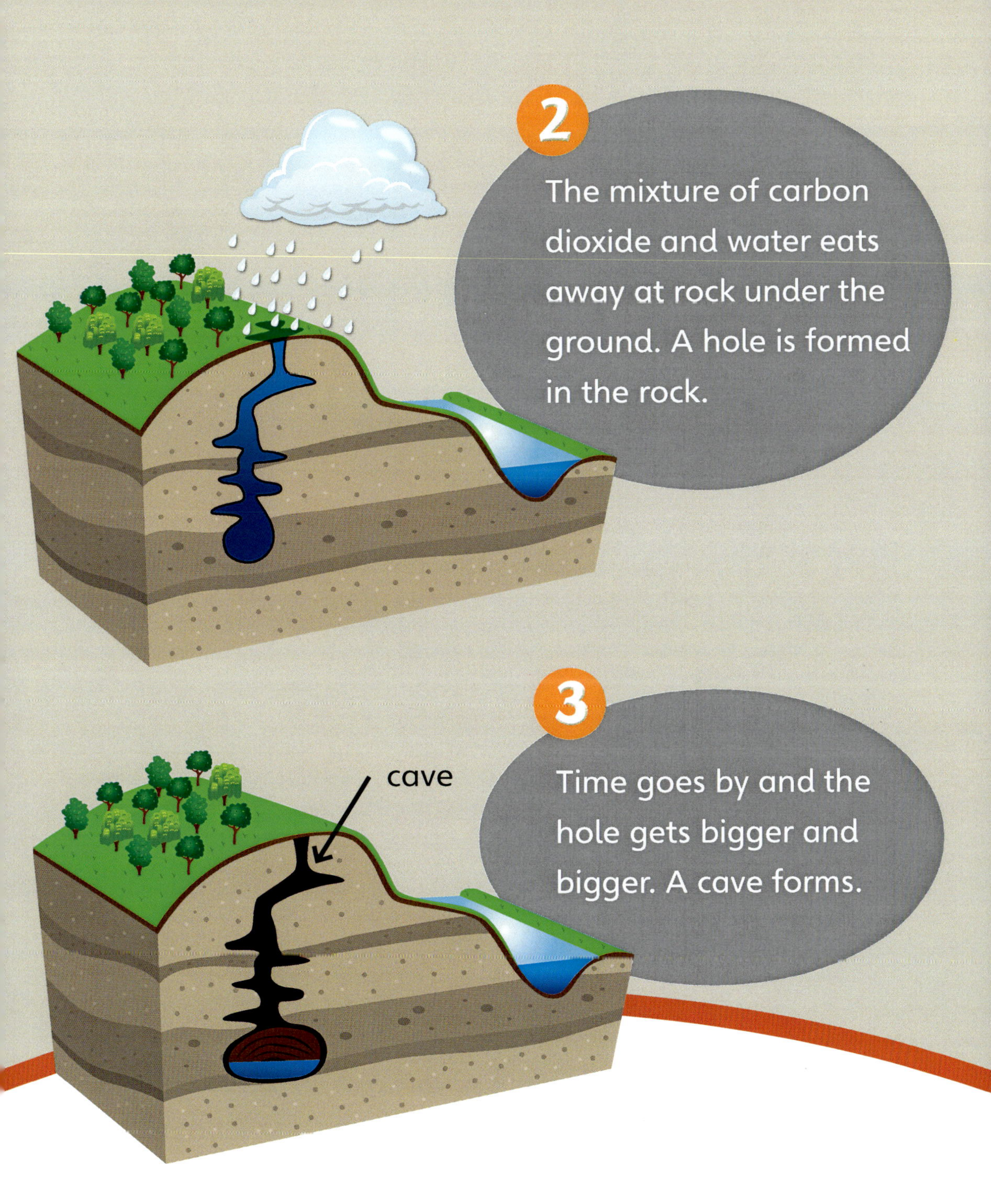
2
The mixture of carbon dioxide and water eats away at rock under the ground. A hole is formed in the rock.
3
Time goes by and the hole gets bigger and bigger. A cave forms.
cave

Some caves are formed by volcanic **eruptions**.

1 A volcano erupts. Hot **lava** comes out.

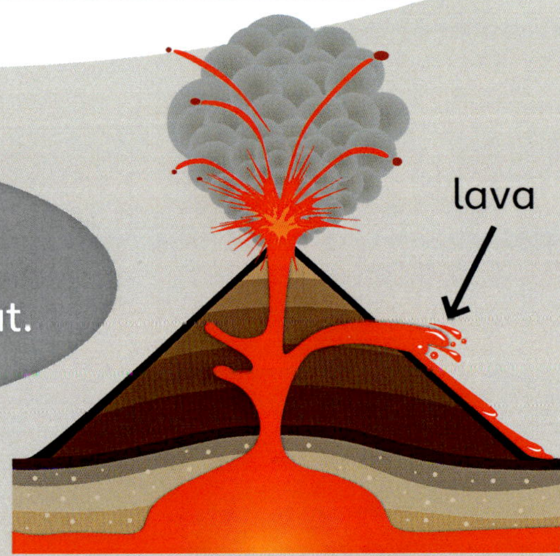

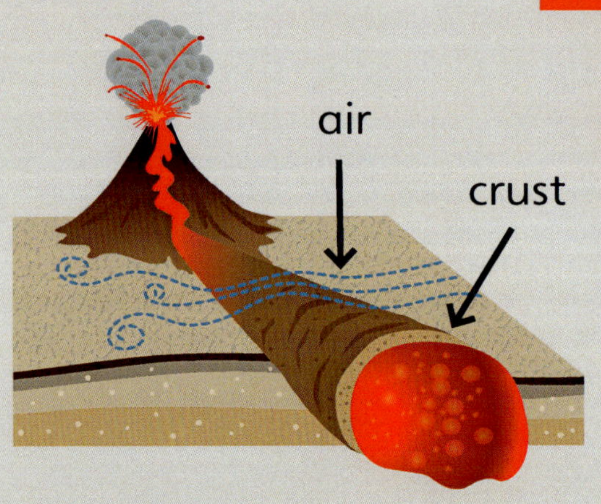

2 Air cools the top of the lava flow and it forms a hard crust.

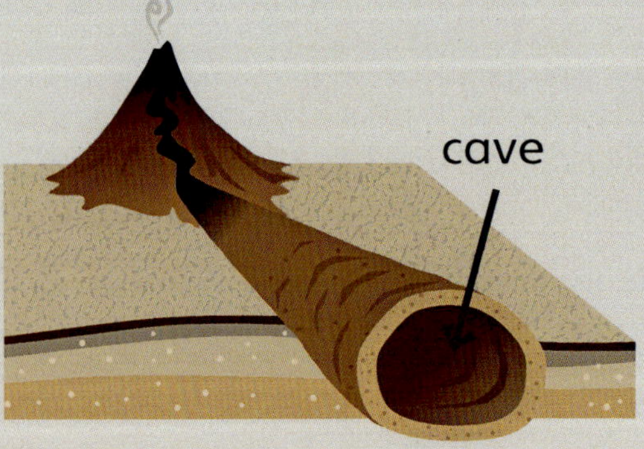

3 The hot lava left under the crust flows away. It leaves a hole and a cave forms.

Some caves are formed by the sea.

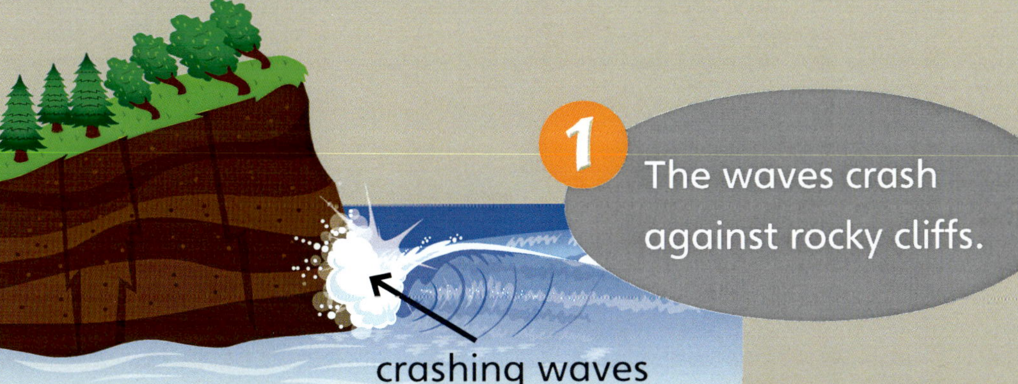

1 The waves crash against rocky cliffs.

2 Weak parts of the rock are worn away, forming a hole.

3 Time goes by and the hole gets bigger and bigger. A cave forms.

Types of Caves

Underground Caves

An underground cave is a large space under the ground. Most underground caves form in a rock called limestone.

Limestone caves are full of shapes. The shapes form when rainwater flows through the ground and drips into the cave. Tiny pieces of limestone get caught in the rainwater. These pieces collect together and form the shapes.

The shapes that hang from the top of the cave are called stalactites. The shapes that grow up from the ground are called stalagmites.

Some underground caves are very big. They are called caverns.

The Carlsbad Caverns are a group of over 100 caves in New Mexico. The largest cave is called the "Big Room".

Name: Carlsbad Caverns
Location: United States of America
Depth: 183 metres underground
Famous for: being one of the largest underground caverns in the world

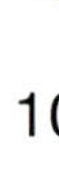

It takes about three hours for all the bats to fly out of the cave.

Many thousands of bats live in one of the caves at Carlsbad Cavern. At night, they all fly out of the cave to hunt for insects. It looks spectacular!

Ice Caves

An ice cave is a type of cave that has large amounts of ice. It is so cold in the cave that everything **freezes**.

Some ice caves are cold because it is cold outside. Other ice caves trap cold air inside even though it is warm outside.

When sunlight shines on the ice in an ice cave, it makes the ice look blue.

Dripping water freezes to form icy stalactites.

There are stalactites and stalagmites in ice caves, too. They are made from rainwater that freezes into ice. The ice makes some amazing shapes.

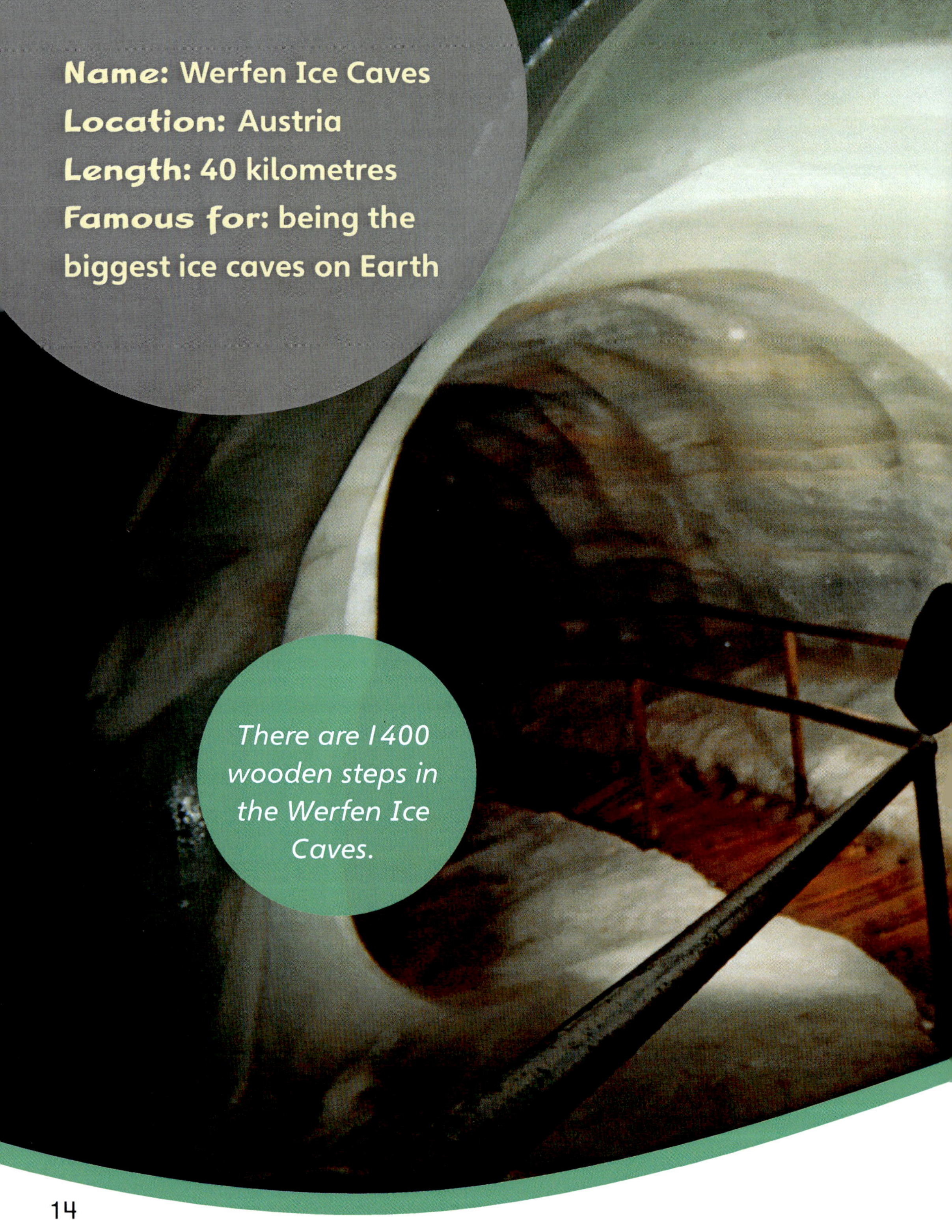

Name: Werfen Ice Caves
Location: Austria
Length: 40 kilometres
Famous for: being the biggest ice caves on Earth

There are 1400 wooden steps in the Werfen Ice Caves.

Cable car

The Werfen Ice Caves in Austria are inside a mountain. You can get up the mountain by cable car. Then you have to walk up a **steep** path to the caves.

Sea Caves

Sea caves are formed by waves crashing against rocks on a cliff. Most sea caves are smaller than other types of caves.

Name: The Blue Grotto
Location: Capri, Italy
Length: 60 metres
Famous for: the blue light in the water

The Blue Grotto looks so blue because the Sun shines through a large hole just under the water.

The Blue Grotto can only be visited in a small boat. Getting into the cave is tricky. You have to lie down in the boat because the entrance is so small!

Fingal's Cave is another amazing sea cave.

Name: Fingal's Cave
Location: Staffa Island, Scotland
Length: 70 metres
Famous for: being made from hexagonal columns of rock

The columns of rock that form Fingal's Cave were made by a volcano. When lava cooled, cracks split the rock into columns.

Living in a Cave

There are all sorts of animals that live in caves. Some are big animals, like bears. Others are smaller, like snails and glow-worms.

Name: Waitomo Glow Worm Caves
Location: New Zealand
Size: 18 metres high
Famous for: being home to millions of glow-worms

The Waitomo Caves are full of glow-worms. Glow-worms are tiny insects that glow in the dark. Inside the caves, there are thousands of glow-worms that look like tiny lights.

School in a Cave

Caves can be used for many things. In China, a cave was even used as a school. Imagine going to school in a cave every day!

Name: Dongzhong Cave
Location: Guizhou Province, China
Size: it easily held over 100 children and their teachers
Famous for: its primary school

The school opened in 1984 and was closed in 2011.

The school had wooden desks and chairs for the children. It even had a basketball court for play time.

Exploring Caves

Caving

Some people like to explore caves for fun. Some people study caves as part of their job.

People need to be careful when they enter a cave. Here are some rules to help you stay safe.

Caving Rules

- *Never go into a cave without an adult.*
- *Take a light.*
- *Don't run or jump in a cave.*
- *Tell someone where you are going.*

People who explore caves need special equipment. This includes a helmet, hands-free lighting and appropriate clothing.

Cave Art

If you explore caves, you might see some cave art on the rock walls. In the past, people drew or painted on the walls of caves to tell stories.

The paint was made with coloured rocks. The rocks were crushed the rocks into dust. Then the dust was mixed with water.

People often drew stories on cave walls about hunting animals.

Kakadu National Park in Australia has many rock paintings made by Aboriginal people.

Some paintings are about hunting animals. Some are about Aboriginal dances. Some of the rock art is many thousands of years old.

Make a Stalactite

You can make your own stalactite at home.
Just follow these simple instructions.

What you need:

- Two glass jars
- A plate
- Cotton string about 60 cms long
- Two paperclips
- Baking soda
- Hot water

What to do:

1. Fill both jars with hot water.

2. Add baking soda to each jar and stir until it **dissolves**.

3. Keep adding baking soda to each jar until no more will dissolve in the water.

Safety Tip

Ask an adult to help with the hot water.

Put the jars in a warm place.

4 Put a paperclip on each end of the string.

5 Put one end of the string in each jar. The string between the jars must have a dip in it.

The water will creep along the string and drips will form in the middle.

6 Put the plate under the string to catch the drips. Now wait for the stalactite to form!

If the drips fall too fast, the stalactite won't form. If this happens, make the dip in the string between the two jars shorter.

Glossary

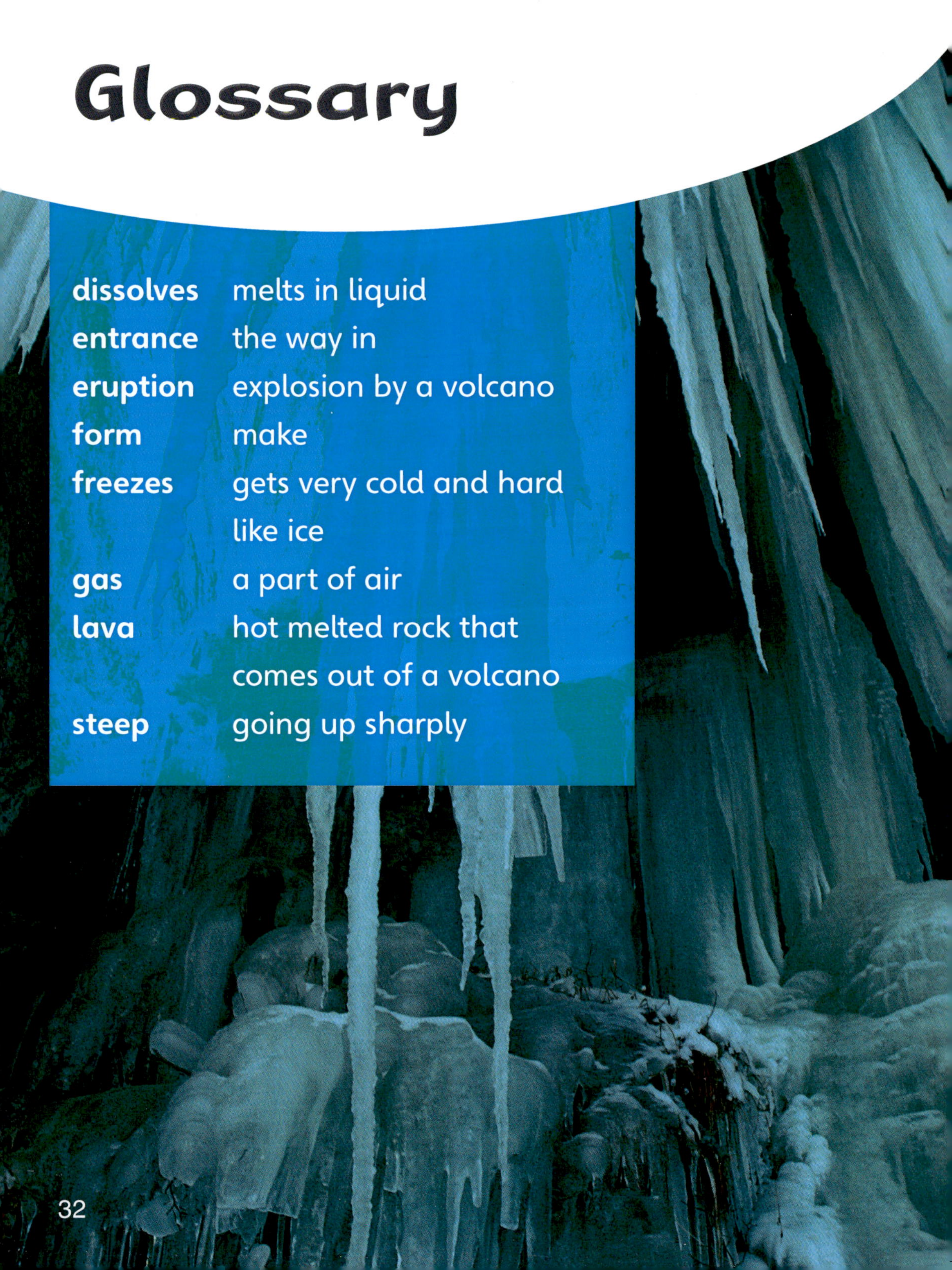

dissolves	melts in liquid
entrance	the way in
eruption	explosion by a volcano
form	make
freezes	gets very cold and hard like ice
gas	a part of air
lava	hot melted rock that comes out of a volcano
steep	going up sharply